ONGOING LIFE

MYRTLE STEDMAN

ongoing life

a universe of mind

SUNSTONE
PRESS

Santa Fe
New Mexico

First edition

Printed in the United States of America

Library of Congress Cataloging in Publication Data

Stedman, Myrtle.
        Ongoing Life : a universe of mind / Myrtle Stedman. -- 1st ed.
            p.   cm.
        ISBN 0-86534-192-3 : $10.95
        I. Title
    PS3569. T3382305   1993
    811' .54--dc20   92-39429
                                                                          CIP

Published by Sunstone Press
            Post Office Box 2321
            Santa Fe, New Mexico 87504-2321 / USA

Acknowledgments

First and foremost I acknowledge the Mind as the creator and the substance of that which it creates. We couldn't even imagine a universe or anything in it without the Mind. It is the Mind that expresses itself and conceives that which it expresses. It is this male and female that is the basis for the production of all that exists.

It is to the Mind and in the spirit of its contemplation that I attribute the end resolves of family and all life situations which enter into ongoing life today and into life beyond the grave, never dying, never forgetting.

TABLE OF CONTENTS

Preface

These poems,
    like so many
    rocks found in
    a riverbed
Need each other as
    in a lapidary
    tumbler
To reveal the
    gems that
    may be found
        in them,
A single one could
    never do
        it.

PRELUDE

January 1991

Dear Sted,

The other day when I called to you, you let me know that you were with me.

Lots of people are going to read about our life together in *House Not Made With Hands*. I know they will love you as I love you. I want them above all else to appreciate all the good we had by being together. I would like them to get the knowledge and feeling that we are still together and in love.

Help me to feel my way into a closer contact with you.

I hear you say, "Of course."

Love you,

Myrtle

GERMINATION:

Questions:Ideas

WHERE ARE THEY THAT
ONCE WERE HERE?

Where are they that
    once were
      here –
Where are they hidden
and how can we reach
    them there?" asks
      Kathleen Raine.
I ask the same
    tormenting
      question.
An architect will
    tell you
  the solution is
    in the problem.
If God is the
      architect
    of all that was
      made
    and is made —
The dead are
    in His thoughts
    couched in the
    creative process;
    in a sketch, a dream, a
    plan of what, where
    or who they are,
      or are to be.
This is where we will
    find them.
  Does this make any
    sense to you,
      Kathleen Raine?

DEPRESSION

Why art thou
cast down
O my soul?
And why art thou
disquieted in me?
Ps. 42:5

A cow might bawl
without knowing
why —
but the bull knows
and satisfies.

Bawl, cry, open up
to that
unknowing.

The church
cut me off
from the very
thing it
wanted me
to know —

That God is my
husband —
that God is my wife.
Divine Love
is my
satisfaction.

Let this new, old
consciousness
be born.

Revel in the
euphoria
of pre-conception;
be one with
the cow.

The reason for depression
is to make
room
for joy.

LONGING

Longing for a coke,
  a cup of coffee,
  a piece of sponge
    cake,
  is the same primordial
    stirring;

Darkness toward light,
  emptiness toward
    satisfaction,
  piecemeal
    toward the whole.

Longing is basic
  to whatever
  one wants.
It is the matrix
  for the mode
    and the mold.

TELEPATHY

The mind is the Creator
    and the created;
        it is everywhere
            telepathically.
The mind is the unit
    and the united,
        the life and
    the living.
All separate individuals
and things
        are separate
            beings
    and things
    of the whole.
The whole is only
    whole in this
        separateness.
Telepathy is the wholeness
    of separate
        meanings
            of the mind.
Telepathically, we can
    be in touch
        with the whole
    and all of its
        parts.

BUZZING THOUGHTS

Buzzing thoughts
    are like flies
    that keep landing
      on your head.

They won't go away
    and are hard to
      be caught
        under your hand,
like the subject
      of automatic
        writing
      and, or, channeling.

A thought came this
      morning,
      that the difficulty
        is that we have
          somewhere
put these thoughts
      in the realm
        of the impossible;
      and they automatically
        stay there.

But if we think
      about them,
    bring them again
    into our conscious
      thought —
and say, "Hey,
      if others can
        do it
    so can I."

It is like buying a new car
      which doesn't
      drive the same
        as the old one.
We consciously
      learn how to
        drive it.
And what we learn
        about it soon becomes
        automatic.

Now in writing,
    I have channeled
      this thought
    into a sensible
      vein.
Listen to its buzzing
    and catch it
      if you can.

FURTHER THOUGHT ABOUT AUTOMATIC WRITING AND CHANNELING
As inspiration or a message from the dead

Automatic writing
      is simply
    a flowing
of communication.
Channeling is simply
     an allowing this
     communication
    to flow,
whether in writing
    or talking.

And where does
    communication
     arise from,
       the quick
    or the dead?

If we think
     of who we want
    to communicate with
     as being dead,
       this is where
    we miss the
      whole point.

We live and breathe
    and have our being
      in God, Spirit.
That is where we are;
    that is where
      the dead are.

Call the name
     of one not incarnate
    and see what
      happens.
If you get anything
     write it down.
If you hear anything
    channel it to
      others.

One can label it
     inspiration
or a message
      from the dead.
Who cares?
      I do. It is both.

Or it is more fun
   to think
   that it is,
     than not.

ANGELS: A DIALOGUE

We have wings,
    but they are
        bent and
            out of shape.
We don't even
    know that
        we have
            them.
A crystal healer
    can see them
        and straighten
            them.
One who can
    feel the energy
        in a crystal,
            can do anything;
                we could, too.
But falling
    from grace
        bent our
            wings;
    made us forget;
    made us dig
        for a living.
We think
    this is the
        only reality.

To think
    and to have
Is beyond our comprehension.
We plug along
    not knowing
        any better

Until someone
    says, "Hey,
        there is something
        better."

I feel at home on
    the ground.

"What's the matter with that?"
Nothing –

Except we are
    fallen angels
        and don't
            know it.

ALTERING THE PATTERN OF ONE'S LIFE

How can one
    alter the pattern
        of one's life?

How did it happen
    that I met a man
        when before
            there was
                no man?

I am asking myself;
    and what is
        "myself"
        that I am
            asking?

I am asking the only
    self that should
        know.

What did I do before
    I met him?

I thought of nothing
    but of the one
        I should
            meet.

This then is how
    I can alter
        the pattern
            of my life.

What then do I want
    to change?
        What is lacking?

What do I yearn for
    in a life that
        is already
            so full?

Where is there a place
    for change?

Why am I not satisfied?

I am lonely —
        for what?

For inspiration!

What is inspiration
    but a wakening
        of the mind?
    An awakening
        of the
            expressive
                side of the
                    mind.

There is my man!
The man every woman
    longs for.
      And mine is right
        here
          in my pen!

Writing, it is said,
    is a lonely life.

No person can tell
    you what to
    write.

But that which inspires
    is the most personal
      of persons.

It is the best of every man —
    that which makes
    the sperm burst
      forth is
        sperm.

That is what inhabits
    the earth,
      fills the ocean,
    climbs the trees,
      digs the channels
        of the earth.

It is the purpose
    of existence
    to manifest
      oneself;
        to be heard

      or read.

    To be silent
    to not do anything
    that would bring change.

Everything is perfect the way
    it is.

Doing things
    has always
      been done.

ON MY TWENTY ACRES

I am like a tree,
      with roots
      spread out
To claim the space
      for my own
      nourishment
            and growth.
Like a tree,
      I put an ingredient
            in the ground
            around me
                  that says,
I love you,
      but don't
            come too near;
      your pollen
            will find me
                  receptive
                        in season
To that ever present
      creative urge
      to "be fruitful
            and multiply"
      things of the
            mind.

GROWTH:

Life Experiences

POTENTIAL REALITIES

When I was a little girl,
        I had an imaginary
                playmate
    whose name was
                Rose.

My family played
        along with me
        and Rose stayed
        with me until
        shortly after I started
                to school.

There I found an actual
        playmate.

Her name wasn't Rose
        but the two of them
        became one and
                the same.

She died that year
        of meningitis
        but I heard her
        say, "I am not
                dead."

My parents said that
        I was a big girl now
        going to school,
                which meant
        learning the difference
                between imagination
                and reality.

I lost two brothers
    and saw their
    caskets buried
        in the ground.

A mockingbird in an
    overhead tree
    tried to console me.

I kept a neat little
    graveyard for
        dead birds
    trying to figure out
    what the mockingbird
        had to say.

A brother and my mother
    died — I had
        enough!

I had become an artist
    and a designer and
    builder of adobe houses.

There was an eraser
    in one hand
        and a pencil
        in the other.

My imagination
    was the probable
    potential of my
        reality.

Lines were erased
    but the idea
    never died,
    just went on
In design after
    design.

"I am not dead," she said.

MOMMA

Momma,
   there is not a morning
    in my life
    that I don't go
     toward my
      closed
      curtains
   without hearing
    your song

"Open darkened windows,
   open wide
    the door;
   let a little sun --
    shine in."

Momma,
   do you know
    that I think
     about you
      a lot?

Do you remember
   how you used
    to ask me
     to thread
      your
       needles

Because my
   eyes were
    younger
     than yours?

How you used to
   say when
  I would drop
   a dish towel,
  "Somebody hungry
   is coming?"

How we used to
  carry water
   three-hundred
    feet
 from the well
  to the shade
   of the ash tree
 to do the wash
  on Monday mornings?

And stop at noon
  to fix a bacon
   and onion
    sandwich?

How you used to say,
  — if it rained
   on the clothes
  while they hung
   on the clothesline,
 that it would
  make them
   smell sweet?

Do you remember
   that when we
      would lie down
        to nap,
     you would see
       dogs and
          clouds,
  an old man's face,
    a magpie
      or something
        else
  in the growth patterns
    in the ceiling boards
      above the bed?

"Do you see it?," you would
       say.

Do I need to tell you
   I love you?

Well, I do.

TO MY DAD

I've so far said
        nothing to you, Dad.
You said little
        or nothing yourself,
                in your day,

You whose ancestors
        came over in the
        Mayflower
                for
        freedom of expression.

Your thoughts as theirs
        (which had been
        behind bars
                in a foreign
                land)

Sprang from
        the root meaning
        of intercourse.

With that you bred
        six of us,
                and that
                        was the
                                end.

Your intercourse
        was restricted
for lack of a condom,
either because they
        were not on the market,
your pride wouldn't let
                you obtain them
or my mother wouldn't
        allow them
                in the house;

Or for lack of a wife
        who would have
        had a dozen of us
        (half of them dead)
if she had been other
        than she was.

Intercourse, she protested,
was for the birds
in their season.

Cold and unwilling
        she stifled even
                your talk.

Other women sensed
        this — and it
        was sad to
                see.

LITTLE SISTER'S COMPLAINT

You used a razor strop
    on our bottoms,
    told us next time
    to clean up our plates
(no matter what
    our mother
    had put on the table).

While she, our mother,
    would have
    gathered us together
    under her
    skirts
    had she dared.

When I became
    older
    I understood —
your Fatherly Love
    was all bottled up --

never mind the
    Mayflower.

Two sisters were born
    eight years apart,
    of the same mother and father;
    yet very different were they.

The eight-year-old mothered;
    the little one resisted
    being born twice.

It was the same between them
    when the older one
    was eighty-eight
    and the little one eighty — this
    set the pattern of the mind —

(This conditioning of the one, trying
    to control the appearance
    and action of the other.)

HAPPY BIRTHDAY, MARION

I asked myself —
    why should I
    wish Marion
    a happy birthday?

It's snowing out.
I've been hemmed in
    for days.
I've got no card.

My birthday
    is tomorrow;
    I can be sure
    a card
    is on the way
    from her.

The words on the card
    will be kind
    and sweet.
They always are.

One time I
Thanked her
    from the bottom
    of my heart
for a generous deed.

And she said,
    "I didn't want
    to do it,
    but I thought
    it was a nice
    thing to do."

What do the
    words on a card
    really mean?

I urge you,
    Marion,
    in my own style —

Have a happy birthday.

TO HIM, MY SON

Didn't I
   tell you
   when you were young? —

Be discreet.
Don't tell
   my guests
this shiny bucket
   which holds the champagne
   is your mother's
      garbage bucket.

They won't
   appreciate it.
it will turn
   their stomachs.
They're supposed to enjoy
   the champagne.

And now
   that you are
      fifty-three,
         we recall
you did tell them.

And your mother is
   a legend for
her brass-and-copper
   champagne garbage bucket.

TO HER, MY DAUGHTER-IN-LAW

I.

If I say
   to my son,
are you going
   to change?
      when he has on
         his jogging shoes
and we are going
   to see
   my banker —

should you
   say,
   And go to
      the bathroom
before we go,
      mockingly?

TO MY DAUGHTER-IN-LAW

II.

Why should
   my motives
      be questioned
and not your own?

Why should
   I be
   on the defensive
      in my own home?

It's the in-law syndrome;
   I hate it!

Be yourself.
Don't talk down
      or up
         to me.

Sure I loved
   having you both
      and your children,
      and your dog
   in my house.

Loved seeing you
      together
hand-in-hand, eye-to-eye.

Nothing
   can be
   more satisfying
      to a mother
      than to know
   her son
   is loved
and his children too.

MY TROUBLE

I am little;
I am meek;
I am easily trampled on.

I am interested only
    in things most people
    don't want to talk about.

I am joyously happy
    with my head in the clouds
    when I am painting,
    when I am watching
        my grandchildren,
        my great-grandchildren,
        my very own sons.

When I am building a house,
    or washing the john
        or writing a book.

I am lonely,
    very unhappy,
    hurt – mad
        when I feel
            cut down.

It is hard for me
        to remember
    that we're all of
        One Mind

That down deep,
        there is only
            the Christ –

The presence of God,
    peace,
    embracing love,
    quiet joy,
    release;

And appreciation
    of my two wonderful
    daughters-in-law.

BELOVED SON

"This is my beloved son in whom
I am well pleased; —"
Matt. 17:5

The father eagle sits on a limb
While the mother in flight is said
To chase their two-year-old away,
To be on its own before she
Broods again.

But who knows what she says
That will sustain him for the
Rest of his life; without them
To bring him his food — to clean
Out his shit from the nest —
To watch over his every movement
Until full grown and full of wisdom?

It must be a great honor
For her to have the last word of impact
And to spend this day alone with
Him, circling in the sky in
A ceremony to be remembered
By mother and son: one that will
Give him the quiet assurance
That he is ready to be on his own;

To look for a mate, build a nest,
To feed and care for his and her young,
To do what life requires of all of
us — to maintain the species —
To love and be loved.

VISITORS

Some people pull you
    out of your depths;

They live on the outside
    of themselves —
        at the tip end of
        their nerves --

They are selfish
    to extremes;
    defensive,
    ugly and impolite.

You go out of your way
    to feed them —
    to bed them
    warmly,

To see that they
    do everything
    they want to
    in the town.

You send them
    home with part
    of your abundance,
    then try to relax —

Take a warm bath,
    bless the hidden
    depths within them
    and wish them
    a bon voyage.

Others
    bring gems,
    thoughts that sparkle.

Sometimes it is just
    the other side
    of "some people."

They leave you
    with a lot
    to reflect on.

You enjoyed
    thinking of them
    in the other
    end of your house.

When you
    walked alone
    with your dog,
    it was nice to think
    of them awaiting
    your return.

They filled
    your coffee pot,
    opened a book
    to share a poem.

There was companionship,
    a feeling of warmth
    because they had come.

This feeling
    they leave with you
    even when they are gone.

Both — or the same
    are welcome
    in your house.

YOU CAME

Larry, you came
    at the edge of winter
    and brought a taste of spring,
Your poetry like
   the flower already open
   while lilacs were still in bud.

You came to me
    for home and shelter,
    a place of quiet
     to work.
You've plucked my brain
   and I've plucked yours
     with mutual respect
     and love

     for a universe resplendent.

Sted, you wanted
    to know
    what were
    his motives?

Your presence he
    felt and was
    glad you asked.

STED

Last night I worked late at the computer here in Myrtle's studio.

I wrote a letter to Willard and unloaded much of the pain that I have been carrying for the last four months. It felt good to write my thoughts since I feel that Willard has not been able to hear much of what I've been saying for the last sixteen years, much less the last four months. I have this hope that reading my words will somehow help him to finally understand why I had to leave the marriage.

When I finished, everything was very still and quiet, inside of me and outside of me. I sat for a long time looking at the books and feeling the energy of this place. Suddenly I became aware of another presence and knew immediately that it was you, Sted.

I felt you were sitting in the chair across from me and that you were upbraiding me in a way for not acknowledging your presence in this house sooner. The message I heard from you was "This is my house too. I helped create this space. And part of what you feel here is me." I thank you for this beautiful space and for helping me to feel sanctuary here. I acknowledge your presence and your energy and your continued influence on those who come here. I salute you.

Margaret Fuller
February 22, 1992

SHE PUSHED A LITTLE
RED WAGON

Traveling to see a grandchild,
I said to myself,
"She will be walking by now."

She was in a cart;
her feet covered
from the eyes of neighbors.

"What's the matter?" I asked.

"Her feet are clubbed.
She will be getting braces."

I inwardly rebelled
and took her in my arms
and fiercely loved her.
She trembled with excitement,
planted her feet
flatly
behind a red wagon,
and

The neighbors saw her walking.

A YOUTHFUL SUICIDE

A YOUTHFUL SUICIDE
(Oh Darkling Youth In Your Casket)

Bright and happy baby
    you were
Your own log cabin
A delight to see on the
    ski slopes
But tell us what went wrong

Plans to be a writer
    of interest
Delighted with the
    meaning of words
Iron bending at school
    to your torch
Shaped in beauty
    to your design
A supportive trade-to-be
    to your writing.

Face drawn now as before
    defiant   saddened still

Let us bury your gloom
    but no part of you
Tell us what to do about
    your disappointments.

The school system, you said,
    is in trouble;
Subjects of value
    dully taught
The Bill of Rights
    you just discovered

But always humiliated
    by right crushed by curse
    and quick forgotten

No different at home
Speaking your mind in
    defense of what
        you thought right
Only got you in trouble, you said,
    and became silent and lonely
Going out at night
    while they were in bed.
Trafficking in drugs
    did that make you a king
Or parental punishment
    stop you?

No,
    because
You put a gun
    to your head.

There is a better way
    to put evil to naught;
By knowing it is nothing
    in the sight of God.

God to us is our very own mind
    perfect in itself
Responsive to all human
    needs.
Then let us see this death
    not unto death
But to the glory
    of God.

While renewing this youth
    in Spirit

Please let us be renewed
    in body and mind.
It is no use for us remaining
    to say
His death had nothing to do
    with you or me –
After just a little light
    has been shed on your
Darkness, Youth, we know
    this to be erroneous.

But this kind of
    Light
On this kind of
    Darkness
Presents an image of the Mind
    you in God's likeness,
Soul unhurt by the blast,
Your illusions and hallucinations
    fled away,
Pure and holy
    Child of God.

And holy, we,
    blest and contrite —
At your bier touch and awaken
    the human concept
    coincident to the Divine

Young man,
    come forth!

IN LIEU OF A SUICIDE NOTE

To Parents:

Tell them
　Their son
　　who could beat his dad
　　in a chess game,
　Could add six figure numerals
　　in his head,
　Could not find principle or rule
　　in an overriding argument
　Though studying each move
　　long afterwards.

He did speak fondly of the
　most argumentative,
Said that he learned
　most from this one
Being already almost
　identical to the other
　in spirit —
　and fondly, too.
Learned early in childhood
　to be silent,
Learned smartly to
　gain his own choices,
Learned when a first choice
　　failed
　to find a second

No matter that it might
　be in reverse
　he made it.

Tell them
　That being able to sustain
　　verbal slurrings
　　or two broken ribs
　(Self-sworn to secrecy already),
　　taking his own life
　　was only a step further
　When it meant saving their lives
　　from the smugglers of drugs
　　had the smugglers
　　been disclosed.

Tell them now
　That cigarettes, liquor, or drugs
　　are reverse-choice
　　stimulants.
　Pure religion
　　is not for monetary gain
　Through cult brainwashing
　　or by speech or threat;
　But that, too,
　　is found
　　in the sepulchre of silence.
　In Spirit — All — Ad infinitum,
　That this true stimulant
　　is a force --
　　a law of elimination
　Of all not good.

Tell them,
   "You find life
      to be a distillation
      from all that is gross,
Waiting due process
      just to find out;
   And that whatever
      they did
   Is now priceless;
      be glad!"

Tell them
   You spoke briefly
      this past summer
      but in those few words
In depth;
      enough for me to say
      that you anticipated
This type of awareness
      past death.

To Brother:

Tell him
"You are the one
      who shouted
      the loudest,
   Got the attention,
      number two boy
      but first.

   First to grow tall,
   First in your classes,
   First out in the morning
      jogging.

You are the one who
      has a lot on the ball.
As to drugs and the pills
      I quit the game
But you gave it up
      first.
In you I am very pleased
      to see the number one boy."

To Sister:
> ask her — using your own cherished
>> *nom-de-plume* for her,
>
> "Newton,"
>
> What takes a sister to her brother's grave
>> To find reality here —
>> To express love without hope
>>> of being heard —
>> To will back my teasing?"
>
> Tell her --
>
>> "The loneliness of my act
>>> ending my own life
>>> to end untold misery,
>>> you feel deeply — cry,
>> But dry your eyes — smile!
>>> feel radiant joy.
>> I am standing by your side.
>
>> "Mission accomplished at seventeen
>>> and past,
>>> wound healed,
>> All teasing gone from my eyes
>> Love Living — Bright
>>> your brother, real."

To Gran:

Great-grandmother
     not by blood
     but by devotion –
Tell her,
     "You changed
          my mother's diapers
          before you
               changed mine.
When my dad was
     a suitor,
You told her, 'That's the one
     for you.'

You have been our
     alarm clock,
Our reminder of
     raincoats;
No one can cook a turkey
     better than you."

Tell her –
     "At eighty-nine your "knees
          are a bother
     Announcing the weather
          change
     Your ears don't
          always hear.
     Though I was not
          your favorite,
     Since you are not
          a respecter of person
          but of deeds,
     I did raise my voice
          so that you
          could hear,

     And account you
          as an administering angel,
     And hurt when you
          hurt
          spiritually."

To Uncles and Aunts:

Distant Relatives
Passers-by and
Lookers-on
And to those faithful stand-bys,

Tell them,

    "You say to yourselves
       or I hope that you do,
    'I don't know what
      I would do
    Should this happen
      to me.'"

Tell them
    "For strength to withstand
      you would turn
        naturally
    To that which is
      in power over all,
    And it would direct you
      to that next power,
    To those thoughts you
      have assigned to look
      after your affairs,
    To your own serious
      commitments
    And to know that others
      around you
      would do the same."

And to Me:

Say, "Grandma,
    you knew
When you saw my hands
    shaking,
Trying to make a metal
    sculpture
For you
    that never got finished –
Just back from a walk
    with your dog
Along the river — to count
    four owls,
Night after night
    papa, momma
    and two babies,
Smoke lingering twice
    in my clothing,
But held your silence,
    praying.

"Praying still
    to know that death
    is a dream,
To know that it
      never happened,
To know that life is
    Almighty Consciousness
    expressed,
That we are the evidence
    that God exists,
That cause and effect
    must be the same,

That we must somehow
    stick around.
Because God *is* —
    we *are*."

Say to me,
    "I came to your kitchen
        the other morning —
You felt my presence,
    you knew
I was pleased with
        your poem
Written at my own
    suggestion.

"Uncovered errors
    disposing
Replacements made
    by affirmations
        of truth
Yet knowing that after
    two thousand years
Of singing and praising
    we will still not
See the body rising
    until we are prepared
To see it happen."

Then say,
    Go on
        with your task.
    I go on to
        mine —

Happy that we
    have
Touched in consciousness.

"Living consciousness
    communicating ideas
    three months in advance
And forever —

"Reaching for and straining
    toward
That consciousness
    so ascended
It neither sees
    nor contains
An element of evil.
    Love's provision recognizes
Our Right — Our Bill —
        Our Fare."

Now I hear you say,
    "This, do, and
        assuage
    My disappointments."

THE MOURNER'S INEVITABLE SELF-QUESTIONING

Oh sorrow,
    why do you
    plague me now,
    months after it
    is done?

Because I was
    blind
    yet seeing his need?

And, slow of tongue,
    when I saw injustice
    done?

Who was I
    to criticize
    criticism?

To whom
    do I owe
    such homage?
To youth or parentage,
    to society?

Youth is young!
    parents have
    never been
    parents before —
    and we are society!

We who
   need to see
   where the unreal
   injustice
   lies

To see that
   only love
   is wise
   and drugs —
   insidious trap,

A blind
   for the boy's
   own unshed tears,

For his own
   misguided
   judgement
   blind, blind,
   blind me!

Where
   then and now
   is my healing thought?

What about
   the lures
   the trips
   into such darkness?

There is light
   in timely speech,
   in poetry.

But anyone
   contemplating
Love's instruction
   is gladdened only
   by those who act;
   (even he,
   you and me)
   Yes —he

He has told
   us
   something
   and himself
   has things to learn

He
   is now
   working things
   out,
   though he shall not
   come forward
   to say so

Our own
   sorrow
   makes us
   know
   even so.

ETERNAL LIFE - HIS LEGACY

I kiss the stone
   which he brought
   me from the river
To uphold my books
   and draw from it
   strength for my writings;
I cry from the depths
   of my heart
   to know what to say!

I have come up
   with this:

What we need now
   is not regrets
Or condemnation
   of self or each other
But to see with eyes
   that see no evil
With His — Life Eternal.

What about the claim
   of indestructible life?
Do we believe it or not
   or have the slightest
   notion of what it is?

We know
   that evil is destructible
But do we know that it
   can only destroy itself
On the grounds that
   God didn't make it?

Or that we dare not
   associate ourselves with
   or ascribe it to others
If we are not to get caught up
   in the destruction
Of its own suppositional entity?

I know that this is so.
   There are thousands
   and millions who do.
There are thousands
   and millions who don't.

That is why we need Christ
   crucified,
Or a gun shot
   to awaken us
To find in the place of evil's
   nothingness,
That which is,
   which was in the beginning!
Let there be light
   and there was light,
And this light is the
   life of man — the
mind of God within him.

The young man and I
     talked about
   an all-good Mind
   that anyone could see,

That it could be God.
      He believed,
      and he could see
That this Mind,
      having no evil in it,
      would be indestructible.
Since only evil is destructing
      and destructible,
What is good remains.

I know this
      meant him;
That he took no thought
      of himself
      in disposing of evil,
Yet sad
      that this distinction,
      that one can be
            separated from evil,
      that one cannot be
            separated from good,
Is not clearly understood;

That body disappearing
      is evidence of this confusion;
That body well and remaining
      or reappearing
      will evidence understanding;

That evil has no part
      in the man of God's creating.
Then damn the evil
      but not the boy,
not ourselves and not each other.

This is what the rock
      that upholds us
      has to tell:
Man is wholly spiritual
      a law unto himself,
      individually expressing Life
And Life providing
      his embodiment for its own
      purposes and development,
With a clearer appreciation
      of what it means to live
Eternally as the mind's own
      imperishable idea.

The youth
      brings us
      peace and joy.

A TREATMENT
One Year After

What is this feeling of depression
    which I cannot rise above?
What is it trying to tell me --
    that there is mental
    work to be done
        for myself
        my son
        for everyone?

Shall I take a pill
        call for help?
I know the law of Mind
It knows my need
        before I ask

I am lifted up
        just knowing this

And all mine are lifted
        with me.

HIS PURPOSE
Second Year After

It is two years
    to the day
    since you shot yourself
    on purpose
(Purpose false,
    purpose pure.)

How long
    shall we
    celebrate
    this passion
    steeped in grief?
Held in thought
    here,

How can you go on
    to see the risen Christ?

(God
    withheld His hand
    for that.)

GONE FISHING

"Come on, Grandma, ya gotta go fishing."
  (flexing his rod and testing his reel)

"We can get enough fish in five minutes for supper.
Wouldn't you like some fish for supper?
It's just the right time of day to go catch them."

"I don't know anything about fishing."

"I'll show you — it's easy,
  and they're gonna be biting."

One cat, two dogs, fishing tackle, two jackets,
  a boy and his grandma —
  gone fishing.

EVOLUTION OF CONCIOUSNESS

This life is so controlled
    by laws, customs,
    fixed ideas
    and the
    AUTHORITIES.

We have stoned,
    burned,
    crucified,
    run away,
    defied

    or completely
    given up;
    become beggers,
    thieves,
    homeless
    dependants.

We become
    spiritless
    creatures

Until fired up,
    inspired,
    empowered,

Find ourselves
    beloved by
    the Mind
    within us.

Then we take
    one more step
    in the order of
    things.

GIFT GIVING

GIFT GIVING

Is a mother rich
    who has nothing
    to leave to her son?

Would there be no competition,
    then, with his wife?

Doubt and fear
    build up
    like a garbage dump,

though hands reach out
    in love.

A MOTHER-SON CONFLICT RESOLVED

It was all about
a piece of land we both loved;
long and narrow,
edged with giant cottonwoods,
a river running at their feet;
a high bluff above and beyond,
bespeckled with green piñon
shadowing all in early winter evening
or blazing strongly in the morning sun.

There is an ancient apple orchard
which a priest's Alsatian gardeners
planted years ago. Withered bare
arms protruding from leafy green,
and an abandoned nursery,
grown tall or bushy -- an open space
between where rows of
gladiolus once bloomed.
After the "glads" were gone
we planted alfalfa and oats
in this field, which waved
in swirls with the slightest breeze.

All this could be seen and felt from
a long sprawling house;
the foothills of the Sangre de Cristo
mountains, too; and big bullhead
clouds and clear blue sky.,

A winding road leading in off
the main road to a turn-around
and parking lot; a studio guest house,
a garden, horses in two pastures
swishing tails, a hay barn, corral
and stable. There were two Toggenburg
milk goats, duck and geese on a pond.

All was designed and put together
    as a family project that grew and grew;
    happily, tiresomely, joyously,
    depressively, by rule of thumb,
    by hit and miss, by father, mother
    and two sons. Tom the elder worked
    like a pro. Wilfred was always
    assigned to picking up scraps
    or gathering watercress — he was
    four years younger than Tom.

Tom, when in his teens, became engaged to
    Marion, who lived across the street.

"What are you going to do with all this land?"
    a friend asked my husband one day.

"We will keep the house in the middle, and
    will give Tom the north end
    and Wilfred the south," he said
    with pleasure and pride. But
    his face fell, and life drained out of
    him, and he lost his interest
        in the whole damn place
    and died shortly thereafter.

Tom, standing by his bride-to-be
    had announced, "Marion and I
    have decided that we will never
    live close to either of our parents."
    He'd taken his cue from the girl's
    unhappy childhood experience; therein
    lay its logic.

Logic spoke through me when I
    said "no" to Tom's question, "Would
    you give the Cottonwoods to Marion
    and me, now that Dad is dead?"

I, too, had a childhood memory of my
parents — giving all they had away,
of dying with nothing of their own.
I keenly felt their self-inflicted
deprivation and promised myself,
that's not for me.

Tom said, "The house and the land are too big
for you. You should move into a smaller
house and give this to us" — still with
no thought to live even with one parent.
"The place is like a rough diamond just
waiting to be cut into many facets —
condominiums, houses, maybe forty-five
units. We could all make a profit."
But I said, "no."

Time came and time went and
the family grew. Both boys were married.
Tom and Marion had three girls —
Wilfred and Edith a girl and two boys.
They all came to the Cottonwoods at
every excuse for a holiday, and I
loved their coming from one year to the next.
Tom told me that he could think of
nothing but to live here on the place.

I forgot one time and made them an offer,
but Marion became apprehensive and
gave Tom and me a hard time. Still
he insisted and asked that I divide
the place into a grid and do it
before they came for Christmas —
poor thing. "What are you going to do
with the land?" Tom asked. "I am just
going to enjoy it for what it is," I said.

Tom came, and Wilfred came. I saw
    deep suffering in Tom's eyes; big
    and brown, a very handsome man, full
    of love and compassion, tall and erect
    but full of cancer. That was his
    last Christmas, though he
    hoped to win to the end; hoped to
    someday build a cancer center on the place.
    "It would give me something to do," he said.
    "I could start now to write letters
    to get money." But his counselor said,
    "No, you shouldn't get involved
    with that big project at this time."

Would giving the land in his name
    for such a thing ease my pain?
    No, I'll turn my thoughts to what
    he accomplished instead of what he
    did not. He left a career as a U.S. Air Force Officer;
    redesigned houses in his area to fit
    modern times and modern wishes —
    updated, expanded, converted junk
    areas into beautiful, useful places. He
    pleased, he inspired, he captivated
    people's love. He remodeled his own
    house -- made it spacious and lovely by an
    indoor-outdoor comprehension and
    view.

He laid a small empire at Marion's feet
    and she bloomed in her own stead.
    Fellowship was legion; he a longtime
    deacon, and she a bellringer in the church
    choir — a very old church where not a
    few presidents prayed within the
    greater Washington, D.C. area.

Though his ashes would rest in the yard, he himself
    looked forward (if he had to go) to a
    renewed environment that he felt he himself
    would make by his own interest and needs;
    his minister and his doctors were amazed
    with him beyond telling, and gained
    imaginative and tasteful ideas from him
    that will help to bring us
                           together.

There is so much to be done —
    to knock down the barriers,
    to lift up the heads, to join in the
    spirit of love, the spirit of joy,
    to look upon our fears with compassion
    until they are no more — swallowed up,
    spewed up to be purified as spittle
    in the sun — and rejoice.

MARION

I probably owe you
    a deep debt
    of gratitude.

It was your unwillingness
    to live with Tom
    on my place

That kept me protected
    from my own
    giving in

To letting Tom
    clutter up
    my land
    with condominiums,
    houses or a
    powered workshop,
Because I leaned
    that way
    once or twice.

NOT SO

Because I have
    written more about
    one son than
    the other,
    is not that I loved
    one more
    than the
    other.

Wilfred stood
    on the sideline
To see what
    Tom and I
    would
    do.

He rarely ever
    entered
    an opinion
    so there has
    been little need
    for a comeback
    regarding him.

And Edith
    his wife --
    though the
    co-head
    of that family
    didn't have too much
    to say —
    just waiting,
    to see if loving them
    I would —
    break the land.

But as far as loving one
    more than the
    other —
    not so.

IN SPIRIT

A CONVERSATION IN SPIRIT

Sted, it is you
        I want.

Come and tell me
    about what you
    are experiencing
        in being dead —

"I haven't been dead —
    I've been alive."

Where —
        tell me —

"With you."

Living in me?

Have I been an extension
    of your life — ?

"Yes —"

So you have been
    doing all these things
        through me — ?

"With you."

I see — I take this
        verbatim
    as true — what then
    about my life?

Do I live somewhere
    else with you —
    Is it as much togetherness
    as my life here
        with you,
        or
        just as little?
I want to realize it
        more fully.
How can I? Was that
        you I was with
        the other night
        in my dream?

When I said, I've never been
    able to call anyone
    'darling,' but now
    I want to call you darling?

Was that you I was with?

Do you wish I would
        forget you?

Am I hanging onto you —
    causing you
        to miss a fuller life —
    causing me to miss
        a fuller life?

You say, "Partly so."

What then? You were
    happy in the dream."

"Stop asking so many
    questions —
    You will know
    soon enough."

How soon?

"Time is of no consequence."

I love you and am
        so grateful to you
    for all I have and do.

Do you love me — or
        is that just one more
        unnecessary question?

"Unnecessary."

I can do no more
    than I am doing —
    and I am happy
        with it —
    but open to more —
        a better awareness
        of you
            and Tom.

TALKING TO TOM IN SPIRIT

How about you, Tom?
Can I call forth your
                energy —
        your consciousness?

Do you understand
        your life
                better
                        now —
        Did I mess it up
                for you?

Do you forgive me?

I feel I have nothing
        to forgive you for.

I forgive you for the
        longing you had
        toward this place.

I wrote about it in
                A House Not Made
        With Hands,
And feel that in this
        it has served a
                worthy purpose.

It is a telling part of
        the book
        and I know that
        it can do the good
        it was meant to do.

Will you accept my
    thanks and
        forgiveness?

I free you from all blame
    and all necessity
    to live another
    life to make up for
        this thing
    that affected us in such
    a deep way.

This is a conversation
        in Spirit —
    but what conversation
    is in anything
        but Spirit?

Have you anything
    to say?

"Read it over again."

All right — I've read it
    and feel you going
    along with it.
    What do you think?
You seem to have to think
    about it further.

I give you time.

Sted said that time is
    of no consequence.

"It is for me."

Oh, I feel your trauma
        yet.

"When I think about it."

But it is not on your mind
    as much as it was
        in life —
    or is it now like
        it was then?

You didn't really make
    up your mind
    to solve the problem
    in yourself.

You know you have to
    look this thing
    squarely in the eye

And decide if you want
    to proceed with it
    or give it up.

Do you want to repeat
    a life with me
    that will even things
    up more to your
        advantage,

Or do you see that
    what you did
    was right
        and complete?

"I still have to think
    about it."

Tom, please — I am
    grateful to you
    for what you did
       for the book.

But now I feel I shall
    be grateful to you
    if you want to
       live with me
        again.

Do something like
       you did, as much
       as it hurt both of us
    the other part was so
        wonderful.

I know if you want
    to carry on with it
    I am more than willing.

        I love you!

Maybe this is what
    Sted meant
    when he said, Time
    is of no consequence.
      WOW!
    Let's do it again!

WITH THANKS TO THE LIZARD

I found a lizard
    on my bed —
  I took a hand towel
    and tried to trap him,
      but he was gone
        in a flash.

In a few seconds
  he peered at me
  from the floor
    by a flower pot.
I tried the towel act again
    and he streaked
      away.

I got a broom
  should he appear
  again — I would
sweep him out the door
  but he was nowhere
    to be seen.

So I propped myself
  against the wall
  on my bed and
    started to read
      my mail —
and there he was
  again on my bed.

He gazed at me
  with pinpoint eye
    relaxed
  and at ease.

I shuffled my mail,
  threw most of it
  into a basket,
  moved about,
and still he lay motionless,
  a hand reach away.

I tried a new strategy,
  got a pan lid —
  sat down again
    and trapped him.

A tail hanging out
  wriggled with
    utter surprise.

I slipped a stiff piece of mail
  under him
  and took him to the yard.

He ran into the myrtle plants
    with indignity.

Who was he?
  And why did he
    choose my company?

What could he have told me
    had I listened instead
    of doing the usual thing
      of putting him
        out?

Then
    I got this –
      "Mom, it's me —
    What did you have
    to do that for?

"It's Tom —
      Tomorrow is my birthday
    I just wanted to be beside you
      to thank you for giving
        me life."
    (three years after he was gone)

God, this is what Tom
    always did;
    thanked me for
      giving him his
        birthday.

And how like him
    to put on a mask.

He was a joker,
    a natural-born
      clown.

But how could he
    do this?

I could swear
    that this was a
      valid experience.

First I thought —
    it's my own
    creative imagination
    and played with that
      idea for hours on end.

Then it took on a more
      serious tone.
    And I opened myself
      wide
    to some truth
    on the matter.

And the truth is
    you are dead
    if you don't allow
    the creative imagination
      to work.

From the beginning —
    all things have evolved
      from and in
        an image.

Thanks to your clowning
      Tom,
    Thanks to your love
      but —

I didn't give you life —
    a life maybe
    meaning a time
To be with us —
    similar to what the
    lizard did.

That almost makes
    sense —
    a collective sense
    of one mind
      in all —

One Spirit —
    yours in its
      combination
    could speak to me
      from anything —

A lizard —
    without being
      – just lizard.

You got through to me
    in the guise of
      the lizard
    but both of you have told
    me the truth.

Don't ask me to prove it;
    collective intelligence
    is a controversial
      subject,
    and the imagination
    has always had to take
      a back seat.

You have given me a very
    happy birthday, Tom,
      with thanks to the lizard.

I know you
    are around
    in your own
      fun way.

THE PROBLEM

I put my hand
    through the car window
    and stroked his beard
        after saying good-bye,

He kissed my hand.

That was Charlie
    your son-in-law, Tom.

It was like saying good-bye
    again to you.

And his sixteen-month-old
    son, again
        like you
    but too little
To know what partings mean.

When they were coming
    this morning for
        breakfast;
    Kathy and Clasien too;
        their last day
    after being here
    for nine years,

I called to your spirit
    and your father's too
    to be with us, as you
        sometimes are —
    but in that dammed
        silence;

Broken too infrequently
    by a wondrous
        joy

Unequaled by anything
    I have ever experienced
      among mundane
        things.

Saying good-bye to those
    I've come to love —
      your son-in-law, Tom,
      and his family,
    is no mundane experience.

I have the same problem
    with them that I had
      with you,
    loving but not giving
    into your basic desire
      to fracture the
        land;
    for you or for them.

I don't feel guilty —
    just hurt
    that it had to be
      the way it was
      and is,
    between you and me
      and them.

When will the good
    to this become
      apparent

When we value the freedom
    it gives
    to come and to go —
    with each other's
      blessing and love.

MY BELOVED CAT

You meowed last night
    in my house,
Though I buried you in the ground
    a few short hours before.

I lay awake in remorse
    for the Christ healing
    which never came —
    for lack of what in my thinking
I could not tell.

You were so loving,
    so beautiful,
    so real,
That I can only know
    that He who created you
    will care for you now.

I am so grateful for your
companionship
    these past twelve years.
When I called, you came bounding
    over tall grass or from a
    soft pillow.

You followed me
    over the trails
    through the woods,
        or from the stove
        to the refrigerator,
from room to room.

You watched me pack
    to go places,
        climbing into my suitcase,
        into the car,
        back to the house,
Until I said,
    "No, Sim, you have to stay,"
Or "Come on, Sim,
    let's be on our way."

In the car
    to bolster your courage
    you mothered the dog —
    licking and smoothing her hair.
You wanted to be with us
    but hated the price —
    a ride in the car.

You yowled halfway there
    or until spent,
    or until I placed my hand
    on your head.
You climbed on the back of my seat
    and wrapped your tail
    around my eyes.
You got under the pedals
    though you knew
    you would be roughly
        spanked.

Finally you'd give in
    and settle down
    until we neared our
      destination.
Somehow you always knew
    before we got there
and paced the car in anticipation.
The dog knew too
    and wagged her tail
    and whined.

You had a boyfriend, Seth,
    and at the family home
you knew the dogs and that they
    would leave you alone
    as long as you behaved;
And that the only thing
    Seth wouldn't tolerate
was when you took
    his favorite pillow
    by the fireplace.

You were loved and petted
    at home and abroad.
In your movements you were
    ever graceful —
Pouncing on the bed
    to help me make it
    or to let me know
    that it was morning —
    time to get up.

You put on a show with
    Pu, the dog,
romping and playing
    in the middle of the floor,
especially when we had
    company.
You two were clowns,
    happy with an audience.

You were a good mouser
    until you got older
    and soft in the head —
Then you watched them
    take over the place,
    though you still had
    plenty of strength.
You sharpened your claws
    vigorously, just in case —
But you never changed
    your mind.

Even in your wasting
    there was intelligence
    and grace,
unfathomable, infinite.
You stood on skinny legs
    to pet me with your tail,

And after death, a meow --
    Not just a healing
    but the ultimate success!

MY DOG, PU

Pu, where are you?
    Come,
  let me imprint
    your spirit
      on this page.

You obeyed my command
  for fifteen years,
  followed me about
  like an extension
    of myself —

Or bounded ahead
  to make my way
    safe.

Surely you are not far
  from me now.

You were a wet pup when
    I got you
  out of your shipping cage
  because you had
    spilled your water
    on the plane.

You whimpered for your breeder;
  for the other ones
    of the batch —

I cuddled you and dried you
  with my dress as you
  sat in my lap on the way
  from Albuquerque to Santa Fe
  and on to Tesuque,
    my home.

"Do you want a dog for show
  or for companionship?"
  your breeder had
    asked me.
"Oh, for companionship,"
  I told her; and that
  is what you have been
  to me for fifteen years.

"I'll send you the first one
  out of her bed in the morning,
  the most spirited one
    of the lot."

And you were always that.
  How can you be
    anything else
      now?

Your soul is what you are,
  not just what you were.

"Is" is present tense.
  Come, let us walk
  over the paths
    of the ranch.

When you knew that I was
  going to put you to sleep,
  you looked over the
  place as though you were
  seeing it for the first time.

You were more courageous
  than I.

When I finally decided
   where I would bury you,
   you stopped at that
   very same spot
   and drank in the feeling.

It is a place beside one of our trails,
   an opening among the
   butterfly bushes,
      on the sunny side
      yet shaded,
      and close to the house.
   Two times you went in there
   and stood and thought;
   where I had never seen
   you stop before.

I knew you knew
   in a way I cannot
      comprehend.

You were in a space
   beyond me;
   in a space
   I simply have to
      know about.

You were and are a Puli,
   a Hungarian sheep dog.
   Herd me to where you
      go beyond me.

Though you protected the house
   with a vicious bark,
   neither you nor the Puli pup
   I got for you to train
      made a sound —

When the kind veterinarian
   and his nurse came,
   you looked at his black bag
      and knew —
   so did the pup.

I kissed you and stepped aside
   to comfort the pup.

You went so softly —
   only a muffled
   weeping was heard.

You would think that you
   had been the doctor's dog
   and the nurse's, too;
   we all cried.

You lay quietly
   in your long, grey,
   curly hair —
   so accepting
      and peaceful.

We lifted you on your pink
   woven blanket
   into my little oratory:
I lit a candle, stepped out
   and closed
      the little gate.

As you lay in state
   through the night,
   I felt your spirit
   collect itself, bless the body
   that it served so long,
      and wait —

The pup lay by the gate
 all night.

At ten the next morning
 the grave digger, a friend
 and I carried you
  in your blanket —
 two talking of other things,
  hard, so they wouldn't
   cry.

I resented the chit-chat
 not knowing its reason,
 and said, "Wait —
the pup wants to know what
 we are doing with Pu."

We stopped —
 the pup put her nose
 within an inch of Pu's
 and withdrew.

We lowered you into the
 two-week-old grave,
 put the two ends of the
 blanket over your body
 and dropped an evergreen
   bough.
 Then the warm earth
 and three more
  evergreen boughs.

My friend, who had steeled herself
 for the occasion,
 said a blessing I had
  always loved:

"There is a wideness in
    God's mercy,
 like the wideness of the sea.
May our life reflect his blessing
 in faith, hope and charity."

Even the pup
 pawing at me now,
 knows more than
 I know, though I am
 her shepherdess.

WHEN HELEN BLUMENSCHEIN DIED

When Helen Blumenschien died in Taos,
    I heard her at that very moment
    say, "Gee, I didn't know
        that it was going to be
            like this."

I was in Santa Fe by the phone
    and received confirmation
    a moment later that she
        had just died.

ONGOING LIFE

MY EIGHTIETH BIRTHDAY

It was the 5th of February, 1988. I awoke, bathed, dressed, walked the dog, my "Shadow," and went to the Big House for buckwheat pancakes with Art and Barb Cassidy. He made the pancakes from a starter that he had made the week before, as his family cook made pancakes when he was a boy. Barb and I both were his guests. She has been staying in town at what Art refers to as the Old Folks' Home. She had a hysterectomy and an eye operation all at once this winter, but was feeling in wonderful spirits for my birthday.

There was an air of renewed courtship between Art and Barb, brightened by the occasion. They love the adobe, but Art likes it cool in the winter and Barb likes to be warm, so she usually leaves the house to him for the winter and goes on a cruise or to Arizona. They have rented the house for over ten years and live in it beautifully. We built it in 1936 and 1937 and lived in it ourselves for ten years; I, my husband, and two small sons.

The joy of having them there and the joy of being there myself for breakfast is a mingling of past and present that matches the beauty of the sunshine in the orchard beyond the windows. The sunshine one can see; the joy is invisible.

The fire crackled in the fireplace in the living room; the coffee warmed our bellies. Then we sat by the fire and talked of old friends. Phil Shultz had a heart attack at the top of the mountain; he got himself down and drove to the hospital and was in intensive care. Dottie's husband, Wes, had a heart attack in Los Alamos and Alice Rosin had died the day before my birthday.

The thought passed my mind — would I recognize the symptoms of a heart attack? Would I have completed a dedicated life when I die, as I felt Alice had done in promoting her father's artwork? This month's *El Palacio* (The Museum's Foundation magazine) was devoted entirely to a history of his life and illustrations of his work. She lived to see it, then died. She was only 81, I learned, by the article in the morning paper. She was so opinionated and worldly-wise, I had always thought that she was at least ten years older than I. As I was leaving, Art made the comment, "Myrtle, you are the youngest 80-year-old I've ever seen; you must be doing the right thing."

At home I had flowers and cards and presents to open, all wishing me a happy eightieth birthday. My grandchildren and great-
grandchildren came. There were telephone calls and a dinner at El Nido with friends. It was a big day and evening.

I went to bed happily tired. About two or three o'clock I awoke with pain in my left arm that spread through my back and to my right arm. A heart attack? Was this what the symptom felt like? Was I that curious that my mind had to make my body show me? I know the mind's artistic creativity, its tricks and trades. I did not have to go to a hospital to see what happened. It carried the trick further and made me extremely tired for about four days — as I had heard Phil's experience had treated him. So what — I played along with it and rested.

In the meantime, two more things happened. I had pain in my lower back and an eye grew dim. I called Barb and thanked her for the lovely breakfast and I called the friends who had taken me to dinner — then finally got Art by phone to thank him.

He said, "You certainly had a big day — how do you feel?" I told him, "I've been resting it off for four days." He just laughed and said, "Well, you certainly know the system and it shows. Barb and I both marvel at the way you climb on the roof and at all the things you personally do to take care of this house and all your other houses and still do your artwork."

"It's my pleasure," I told him.

"Well, many happy returns," he said.

TITLE

My title is
  "Ongoing Life"
But here I am thinking
  of dying.

I've had a lowgrade
  infection in my
  left eye

And I am under a doctor's
  care — so I
  do what he tells
    me to do
But I am not shaking
  it off.

I accomplished things
  I had to do
    by yesterday's
    date.

So I went to bed today
  to shut my
    bothersome,
    scratchy
    eye.

I didn't want
  to think —
  just sleep.
    I slept for hours.

The telephone ringing
  woke me finally
  and demanded
  that I use my
    mind.

It was flexible
  but I wasn't.

My lungs hurt
  from shallow
    breathing

My backbone
  and shoulders
  were stiff.

And I began to
  realize
    that if you don't
    use them you
      lose them.

So I began to use
   the one thing
that worked
     to work the
       others.

They worked
   but reluctantly

This is the way
   I could die
   or become
   a vegetable
     I thought.

I better decide which
   while the mind
   still works.

So I have chosen
     to trust
That the mind has
   a secret
   up its sleeve
     that will preserve
me in itself.

This happened once
   spontaneously —

I was lying on the
   bed and I
   was a foot above
     myself

My mind was in
   the form above
   looking down
     at the form
     below
as though I had
   eyes in the
     back of
       my head.

FOR MOTHER'S DAY

For Mother's Day I received
a call from
my sculptor son,
my orthopedic surgeon
son,

Who wished me a
happy Mother's
Day.

"Yes," I said,
"I was just
thinking how
I had been the
mother of
two sons."

"And you are the grandmother
of how many
children?"

"Six," I said.

"And how many
great grandchildren?"

"Seven."

"There is your
re-incarnation,"
he said.

"Well, I don't know
   about that.

"Both you and Tom
   were born
   with your own
     personalities,
And all the grand
   and great-grand
    children
     too."

"Yes, but with your
     genes —
   Think about that."

"I'll go along with that
   only if you
   can figure out
     how those
       genes

"Have kept up
   with me.

"Come to think of it —
   I know they
    have,

And this bears out
   What I have
     always thought
     about genes —

They are telepathic —
   They know
     what goes
     on in
       whose
         mind.

But wait a minute —
   this accounts for
   a collective consciousness --

An individual identity
   has its own
   re-incarnation

Which is one
   with the
   collective;

All this I thought
   to myself —
   After talking
   with my
   son.

COMPLETION:

Answers: A New Beginning

WAR AND PEACE

Tonight, January fifteenth,
    nineteen-hundred
       ninety-one,
I turned off the news
    — all about
      the speculation
        of war —

silly questions
    with no
unequivocal
    answers.

I turned to my own
        thoughts,
      worn out ones
in view of all
    this.

I struggled with them
      for a couple
        of hours,
gave up —
    and turned
to the thought
      of the Allness
        of God.

What peace!
    All the threat of war —
    the struggle with,
    slippery speculation
        vanished.

Free!
    Have you ever
      tried it?

It is not just
    sticking one's head
      in the sand.

It is a real
      clearing house
      that reaches to the
        ends of the
          earth.

It can cause
    a moment
      of relief
    or a hundred-year
      quieting.

Peace
    instead of
      war.

This war was fought and won
    in forty-two days.

THE ALLNESS OF GOD

In the allness of God
nothing is excluded.
How could it be
allness
if this were
not so?

Then violence;
drugs, murder,
and theft
are all part of
the scheme --

All fermentation,
a cleansing, vinegar
process.

But it is this stage
that makes,
All,
worthwhile.

Why else --
would we
fight wars
against this
or that --

Except to maintain
the consciousness
of the
    Allness of God.

DESTINY

We have a destiny;
    the creative mind
        demands it of us.

We are working
    elements of
        the mind.

We work to
    reproduce
        its kind;
        its image
            in mind.

In love we create
    that which we love;
        this is our destiny.

Be that whatever
    it may.

REST

This morning
    I awoke with a
        clean
            feeling
    like a bucket,
            empty;
    nothing pressing
        its sides,

A delicious
        emptiness,

A quiet patience,
    — no anticipation.

Primordial rest —
    gate to the
        morning.

BIRTH

We are not put here.
We came here
of our own
volition:

To be — to do
and enjoy,

To carry on
what we did
before
or to try a new
thing
evermore.

We were here
in the first ray
of light
comprehended
by darkness.

We are the image
of what we
can imagine.

We are the He and
the She
of our own
creation.

We bring
our past
to the present.

And in our dreams
we form
the future.

We are the invisible
means of our
own
being.

Our birth is the
natural
result
of our
dreams.
We are that
spark of light
hidden but
for a time
in darkness.

We are the imprint
of that darkness
too.

This is why we
can see ourselves,
and be
ourselves,

When we are
born.

MARGARET, THOUGHTS I HAD AFTER YOU LEFT

You said you think of Jesus as God — or the
Christ as God — you are right — but none of
us have an existence apart from God.

You mentioned dropping an overcoat — there is
no overcoat — there is only spirit,

Materialized or visible spirit, or invisible
spirit that has faded into another form.

The whole universe is self-contained pulsating
life — this is our image, conscious of what we
are doing, going from form to form.

We are all a form of the Mind's energy.

THE HAVES AND THE HAVE-NOTS

The haves
    are the naturals;
        they long for
            and have.

They set the day
    of pouring
        and the time
            to mold.

The mind knows
    what they need
        before they ask,
            waiting.

The have-nots prolong
    this waiting,
        not knowing.

And the pouring
    cools and hardens
        into nothingness.

THE MIND

I love the Mind
    with all my heart
        and soul;
    it is my
        God.

My gate is open —
    open wide
        to receive its
            blessing.

It is my husband;
    I am its wife.

It is the word;
    I am its ear.

It inspires me.
    I produce that
        which it
            inspires:
    a painting
            or writing;
    a child
            or a house.

I am its counter-point;
    It cannot be my God
        without
                         me.

LOVE

God loves you and me.
    He can't do anything else --
        anymore than
            water can

Stop filling holes in the ground
    when it rains.

It is as simple and as
    exciting as that.

Itself in everyone --

Itself in everything --

A crying,
    laughing
        Love

A love that says,
    "Look at me.

I am everywhere --
    In beauty,
    In sorrow."

Yes, most of all
        in sorrow --

A sorrow
    that cries
        in the depth
        of my soul

For loved ones
    gone by,

For loved ones
    nearby.

That had or have
    this self-sufficient
        Love.

NOT JUST A SYMBOL

Is marriage
        a symbol
            of
        Divine Love?

    No.

But it should
        tell us
    that to be Divine
    calls for two
            things —

An expressive
    and a receptive
        attitude.

The Mind's own
    interaction
        is the Spirit
    in which
        we live.

In marriage
    two take a
        vow
    to preserve
        this Spirit.

Spirit needs
    no vow
        to preserve
            it

It just is —
    everlasting.

A marriage
        can break
    though it is
        meant
    to last
        "until
            death do
            us part" --

    a symbol
        of the eternal
        nature
            of Love?

A marriage
    is wondrous
        indeed,
    if it lasts --

And if a marriage
    comes anywhere
        near
            being,

"In our image —" Gn. 1: 26, 27
In the image of the
            male-female
            Mind,

IF THE MIND IS THE CREATOR

Or in the end,
   comes to
      the understanding
         of this
            connection

Then, more important,
      and the thing
         I have lived
            to say,

And would be in
         remiss
         if I didn't,

Marriage is not
      just a symbol
      of an image
         of love.

It is, or should be,
      the real thing —
         Mind united
            in Love.

If Mind is the Creator
      and the stuff
         of which everything
            is made —

We don't lack for
      anything.

MIND IS NOT JUST IN OUR HEADS

The mind is not just
    in our heads --

It is universal.

Scientists and physicists
    knock themselves
        out,

To find two interacting
    waves which Einstein
    declared started with
    the Big Bang.

And which are still interacting
    throughout
        the Universe.

When they do put a finger
        on them —
    and they will,

They will find
    that the Big Bang

And all the waves
    it put out

Was caused and is the
    effect still

Of the coitus the two selves
    of the Mind accomplish
    in their on-going and
    ever-renewing and re-
    birthing consciousness
    of one another —

In waves of joy.

SEARCH THE HEAVENS

Scientists search
    the Heavens
        for signs
            of intelligent
                beings,

While the earth
    is teaming
    with intelligent
        beings
            that

We are only beginning
    to understand.

But searching the Heavens
    will speed this
        up.

FOR A GRAND-DAUGHTER

Dear Marilyn,

I could feel your letter coming and I am glad they keep coming. Thank Michelle too for her water colors. I noticed in looking at them how well she was brought out the color in the figures and objects instead of all over the page. She is a good little artist.

I heard the tapes you sent. The woman speaks well and I know she does a lot of good. As I heard them I did a lot of mental editing. The most valuable thing Sted did for me was his mental editing of what I thought and said. He was widely read and could beat me down to essentials, and still does, so that I could write this just the other night.

There is Mind

It is expressive
                    } Creative
and receptive

It is male
                    } Productive
and female

Creativity = Productivity

It is wisdom
                    } Intelligence
and it's understanding

It is action
                    } Spirit
and reaction

It is inhaling
                    } Alive
and exhaling

It gives of itself
                    } Love
and it receives
    of itself

In these aspects it is God

God is nothing
    but this

And this is everything
    both animate
    and inanimate

It is formless
    and it is form

It is energy
    and it is matter

It is personal
    and it is impersonal

It is all there is

There is no other God

There is no other anything
    but this is —
        everything.

Love you,
Grandma

THE VOID

I am that emptiness,
    that bride-to-be
        of the spirit;

I am its darling,
        waiting,

A void as deep
    as infinity
    that only infinity
    can fill.

I am that nothingness
    so important
        to that which is.

I am the complete
    submissiveness;
Without me nothing
    is moved.

I am woman.
    I know
        my power.

TIME

Now I am facing my eighty-third birthday.

Time they say is a clock device: the past, present and future are all here and now.

This is a quiet morning before sunrise. The birds are eating at the bird feeder on the portal while I am finishing my oatmeal and raisins, toast and coffee.

I share my big table with pages and pages of writing — orderly spread, from one end to the other. The fire is quietly talking to itself, and all is well with me.

Shadow wants out to bark at the beautiful young coyote that pranced right past the back of the house and has stopped to paw out some fallen apples from the snow. A dozen magpies have swooped from the air to the ground around her, waiting to pick up any morsel she leaves. In their impatience they take to the air hoping to alarm the coyote to leave before she eats everything of the apples. The coyote looking up sees nothing to fear. When she finally moved away they flew in to pick up the crumbs.

Now the sun has come up and the small birds are sitting on the pinon branches above my window, fluffing their feathers.

When I think of time, I sometimes feel it is taking me with it which gives me a disquieting feeling in my chest.

This morning I didn't wake up with this feeling. I woke with the feeling of gladness and expectancy. And it came to me that all of the past is recorded in the structure of our cells and our bones. An archaeologist can read these bones and a biologist can read our cells, reading the intangible in the tangible, while we in life are forming modifications that will appear tangibly in the future. What they are reading is the development of the psyche, the creative in the created.

I asked that feeling in my chest, of another day, what it had been trying to tell me. It came to me that it was the creative urge trying to open up and bring about a possible probability into the foreseeable future — a new painting — more writing — a renewing of body and mind to add to the ongoingness of life and time.

I AM MYRTLE

I am Myrtle.
Everything in my life
is adjusted
to that name.

As Myrtle,
I came.

As Myrtle,
I will remain.

My life is grounded
to the single
purpose
of being Myrtle.

I scatter my wits
when I try to be
anything else
but Myrtle.

In the name Myrtle
is all I need.
It spans the
whole universe
of energy;

It selects
and collects
ideas of what
I shall do
With the mind.

I am happy
and joyous
With the name
Myrtle.

It gives me a unique
way of expressing
the whole.

The whole
is compressed
in my name,
Opening limitless
possibilities.

However divine
or mundane
my job,
The finished product
carries the
undeniable
stamp of
Myrtle.

The name Myrtle
goes on my
paintings.
And to my writing
I sign, Myrtle.

Who else should
claim what I do?
Who else but me
can paint
what I paint,
or say
what I say?

NORMAL LIFE

PAIN AND REST

Sharp pain traveled
　　from left to right
　　across my forehead,
　　　　into my ears and
　　　　　　down into my neck.

Every pulse was a base
　　drumbeat --

My thinking was fuzzy
　　and I was writing
　　about it instead
　　of calling my doctor
　　　　(until later.)

When I did — he looked at me
　　over the top of his
　　thick-lensed glasses

And said, "temporal-arterialitis,
　　ve-ry serious,"

Waves of ripples
　　traveled from
　　head to foot
　　　　as water on a
　　　　　　puddle
　　　　　　driven by wind.

Lower back pain
　　and in my buttocks
　　wouldn't give up.

Then in my upper back
　　for days and days.

Small flashes of
　　purest light
　　and patterns of
　　darkness appeared
　　in my inner sight,

Then over-all patterns
　　of red and black.
Then all let up —

And I was free.
It thundered and
　　lightninged,
　　　　It rained.

I stood at the door
　　and enjoyed
　　　　the blasts
　　　　　and smelled
　　　　　　the ozone.

The wind swung
　　every cottonwood
　　　　leaf.

Then the sun sparkled
　　on everything.

I praised the beauty
　　and security
　　of my home.

I appraised the
　　companionship
　　　of my dog —

And the kindness
　　of a friend.

I enjoyed doing
　　every little
　　　task

And lay down
　　often to rest.

REST IN ACTION

I've had two long
   months of rest,
   day and night,
     yet I am not
       rested.

Now I realize
   that this type
   of rest
   is no good for me.

It would stop
   all activation.

I need to be fired up again
   by some inside or
     outside
       inspiration.

My ticker
   needs to be
   wound up.

What made it unwind?

Thinking of my age?

Telling people how
   old I am.

Listening to predictions?

Succumbing to the
   usual prescriptions —
   falling in line.

Where is that
   creative urge
   that brought me
     to life in the
     first place —

That commitment
   to join in the fun
   of creating the images
   that appear in
     the mind?

Where is that resting?

I am questioning,
I am looking,

I am listening.

Where is that hollow place —
   that hole under a bush
   from which all things
     come forth?

What lies inert there?

I can feel it filling
   that space

It matches my temperature –

It feels so comforting
    and right
        to be there --

It stirs up a memory.
    "It is good for you,"
        it says

And slowly rises to a
    high place —
        a crescendo.

It is done,

I am spent,

I am relaxed,

    And rested in a
    place of prenatal
        grace.

DON'T TROUBLE YOURSELF

Don't trouble yourself,
Or don't trouble me
    by asking or wondering
    why I haven't been
        healed.

Time is of no consequence
    when one is experiencing
        and learning
            about life.

PATIENCE

There has been something
   strange about the
   way I've felt about
     this health problem.

And I've just now
   put my finger on
   what it is.

I was disdainful of my
   dad, years ago,
   when he had a problem.

He would respond and
   be alright when we
   were alone.

But when anyone else
   came along
     he would put on
     a show of being
       in pain and miserable,
       and was, I am sure.

I know that I could
   have handled my
   problem except in a
   way I've been
   doing the same thing
   he did.

So, Dad, forgive me
   for considering you
   weak and unfaithful
   to what we were doing
   when alone.

I don't understand
   and I do understand
   that this sort of thing
   calls for patience of
     ourselves and each other.

What actually happens is,
   we can call all pain and
   misery back in preparation
   to tell the doctor or others
   how we feel when asked.

This should be telling us
   that we can put pain
   and misery
     clear out of our
       mind —

And this, based on the
   assumption
   that

The Mind by itself
   has no problems —

And this is where that
   being alone
   comes in.

WHAT IS THE INTENT –
I ASK MYSELF

When your children
   begin to look
   almost as old
  as you do,

And their children too
   are growing up;
To live forever
   Or are you through?

Your house is all paid for
   (long ago) and
Your bills are all paid,

You have reached
   the place of
      independence
      you have worked
     for.

You have built houses,
   developed the
     land,

Covered walls with your
   paintings,
Written words by the score —
   throwing more away
     than keeping.

What is the idea —
   give up or
     go ahead?

I've looked into the
   future for
     reference –

It is all veiled,
   hidden or conjecture.

Why, for Heaven's sake,
   if there is
   more there?

THE INTRIGUE

I've been so interested
    and anxious to know
    just how life goes on
        after death —

I think I have set myself
      up to find out.

Our whole universe
    seeds, blooms, casts its
    seed and dies —

But that is only what is
    made manifest;

The thing in back of this
    is the intrigue.

CAUSE

I am all swollen up
        from head to foot.

I've racked my brain
        as to what could
                have caused it —

                Negative thoughts,
(of friends concerned
        only with
                my welfare?)

(Thoughts that I am doing
        more than I should?)

I went over these
        one by one,
                        then,

I switched —
                        Could it

have been something
        I ate?
                        Strawberries!

That's it, I ate half a
        package of frozen
                strawberries
        after avoiding them
                for years.

Why?
                        Because someone said,
        "They will do that to you."

But, in either case —
        looking at it on paper
                I can see

That it wasn't what
        my friends said
                about doing
                        too much,
Or eating strawberries,
        but that I let
                these thoughts
                        enter my
                                head —

Some would say,
        "Hypnotic suggestion,"

But I would prefer to
        keep it in line
                with what I've
                        been saying —

That what is expressed
        and conceived
                is always
                        cause,

And there is no other
        cause.

THE LATTER END

Older wisdom in me
        must be laughing
            at me.

I've been like Job
        telling God how
            good I've been,

Yet suffering this and that.

First, the artery problem
        that sent me to
            the head-scan
                machine.

There, I was given a paper
        with a lot of questions —
            name, date of birth
                and so on.

And at the bottom of the list
        "Are you wearing a —?"
        "What's this," I spelled
        it out to my friend, Dora,
        who was standing by,

And who had taken
        me there because
        she knew all the
            ropes and answers,

Having been there,
            herself, before.

"Oh Myrtle," she said.
        "You don't need to
        answer that one;

It's a thing you wear to
        keep from getting
            pregnant."

Me, at eighty-three,
        was going through
            my mind...

And I looked at the
        young male attendant,
        sitting on a stool,
        elbow on the counter,
            chin in hand.

He, too, was laughing —
        without making
            a sound.

And I laughed back,

Then we walked down
        the hall, almost
        hand-in-hand,
        to the machine.

Dora found a friend,
        a nurse who
        promised to rush
        the results to
            my doctor.

But there was nothing
        there to see except
        something missing,
        "a little brain tissue,"
            the doctor, said.

Then one night four months
  later, I vomited all
  night long.

"Ah, shucks," the doctor said.
  "Bring her to the hospital
  emergency room."

But I didn't want to move,

And didn't, until afternoon.
  With hair down and
    in gown and robe,

A wheelchair met me
  at the curb.

And I was parked
  before a long mirror
  in the doctor's
    examining room.

I looked like a witch.

It made me want
  to retch.

The doctor came in
  and said, "Well, are you
  going to the emergency
    room?"

"We wanted you to come in
  this morning —

We can't do anything
  until we know
    what's the matter."

I almost vomited
  in my lap.

A nurse quickly handed
  me a little kidney
  shaped thing.

I held it up to the doctor
  and said, "This has
  changed my mind.

When I want to throw up
  I need a bucket."

I was wheeled through
  the wind and cold
  over asphalt
    to the hospital
    emergency room,
  green thing still in
      hand.

There I spent three hours.

I was switched from
  wheelchair to bed —

From bed, to bed-on-wheels —

From, "Do you think
  you can stand
  on your feet while
  we get a picture
  of your chest?

"Hold – breathe",

Then lifted back onto the
  waiting wheeled
    thing.

And back into the
  emergency room.

I forgot to tell you about
    the oxygen.

"Did it help?" the doctor
      asked, among
    other things.

"I guess it did, if that was
    what it was supposed
            to do —
I feel fine."

There were a dozen girls
    in and out —
    asking my name
    and date of birth,
    writing it down
         on paper

While wiring me up
    and turning on
    and off switches.

The doctor said (and he was not
    my regular doctor
    who sent me over
    (but a substitute), "I don't
    think you have arterialitis
    — it doesn't fit."

A neurologist had said
    the same thing.

"What you have now,
    the substitute said,
    is a forty-eight hour virus,
    and you are already
    into it twenty-four hours.

Go home and drink
    lots of liquids."

After I got over that
    having called in
    a day and night
    person to clock
    liquid intake every
      half hour,

I felt fine,
And paid her five hundred
    and thirty dollars
    for her time.

Dora had arranged
    for her to appear
    out of nowhere
    when I yelled for
      help.

This is when the spirits
    within me must
    have said, "She feels
    fine but still doesn't
    know where her help
    is coming from,

Or when to quit.

Let us give her a pain
    in the belly — and
    make her left leg
      like jelly," another
               said.

So my left leg
    flopped along like a
    rubber thing — and
    the pain in my belly
      had me doubled
      in two.

My doctor prescribed
    more lab tests —

Then called me at 9 P.M.
    to say that the tests
    showed me to be
        exceptionally clean.

"But if you don't mind
    would you come in
    and have a couple
        of x-rays taken?"

I spent two hours and a half
    doing that,

And wouldn't you know,
    they came out clean.

"You are puzzled, aren't
    you?" I asked my
    doctor and he said,
    "Yes, I am."

"They still don't know,"
    my body mind
    must have smirked.

"Let us put a film
    over her eyes
    so that she can
    only half see."

And through this film
    I picked up my
    bible and read:

"I know that thou canst
    do everything, and
    that no thought can
    be withholden from thee."
        Job 42:2.

And I knew that all
    these ideas of what
    was wrong needed
    to be explored.

Then verse 4:
    "Hear, I beseech
    thee, and I will speak:
    I will demand of thee,
    and declare thou unto
        me."

And I knew that this intent
    is the basis of body
    language, hospital
    gear, doctor's diagnosis,
    pills and everything.
        And took heart
    when I read:

"So the Lord blessed the
    latter end of Job more than
    his beginnings."
        Job 42:12

AN EXALTED VIEW

One of Dr. Deepak Chopra's
    stories about a patient
    who accomplished
    a higher state of
        consciousness
        was

In a depressed mind
    he sat on a park bench
    and closed his
        eyes

And inwardly saw a sky
    with storm clouds
    passing
        by

He let the storm clouds
        go

And searched for a
    spot of blue --

There he fell into its
        mood.

And when he opened
    his eyes

It was to a new and
    exalted view.

MEDITATION

I was meditating
    in the style of
    Deepak Chopra

Quieting the usual activity
    that goes on in
    the mind —

Letting silence envelope
    me, that potential
    out there and
    within.

Just waiting to be
    motivated in my
    behalf, it dropped
    all former acts and
    the conditions they
    imposed.

Purity itself was all
    that was before
    me.

A powerful nothingness
    and a powerful
    something,
    together as one,

Filled me to the brim.

STED IN MY DREAM

I had a dream
    about Sted
    last night.

I was where he was
    and I wanted
        to stay with
            him

And be his wife.

I was telling him
    that it made
    no difference
        that he was
        older than
        I was.

But he turned
    and walked
    away from
        me.

I noted that
    he was wearing
        a white suit

And I saw that it was
    too big for him;

It occurred to me
    that it was
    what I had
        robed him
            in –

And that it's too
    much for him.

All he wanted and
    wants

Is a normal
    life.

I, too, want only
    a normal
    life

Enriched by
    all I've
        written.

A NORMAL LIFE

My writings are
about what
I call a normal
life —

With its ups and downs,
its struggles and
successes —

With its heartaches
and joys
in resolves —

And when I look
out on the
billions of
people —

They just look like
so many Myrtles,
Steds, Toms and
Wilfreds, Marions
and Ediths, children,
grand and great —
grandchildren.

And I love them
all —
and the world
about them.

And all life,
normal or
otherwise.

Coda

STORIES

There is a story about
  two brothers
  who were walking
  in the woods
    one day.

One suddenly stopped
  and halted
    the other
  with the statement,

"This spot, right here —
  I was hatched
    in a nest
    here
    on the ground."

There is another story
  about an Indian
    who was crossing
    a bridge
      one night.

A car hit him:
  it was dark
    and he had
      no light.

The people in the car
  were dazed
    and all shook-
      up.

They saw that they
  had hit a man
    and broken
    his leg.

Before they could
  get him into the
    car
  and off to the
    hospital,

The Indian
  turned into a dog
  and took off
    for the Pueblo
  four miles away –

On three legs.

Now my story —
  or the story
    about Tom

Who was crazy
  about the place
  where he grew up –

I've described the
  place
    and told you
  at length

How he loved this
    land
  and his struggle
    with me;

And my ache
over him
and how he
died.

So you shouldn't
be surprised
when I tell
you,

He has been on the
place at-one
with a she
coyote.

She walks by the
house in
broad daylight,

Stands a few feet
from me
unafraid
and at
home.

She knows every inch
of the ground;
the river
in back,

The cottonwoods
and the arroyos,
the road and
the neighborhood.

She is beautiful,
self poised
and at peace.

I have no doubt
in my mind
that she is Tom's wish
to be here,
satisfied,
(no more or no less than that:
but whenever he chooses)

And as he slept
when a boy
in a sleeping bag
out-of-doors
with his dog near by,

She sleeps in a den
beneath cottonwood
trees
under a brush pile
along the river bank,

And awakens in the morning
at the sound
of my call.

And since this is
Good Friday
I'll tell you still
another
story.

You know it well
in your own
way —

But maybe not the way
I'll tell it,
or the way it can
be read.

There was a man
  born in a most
    unlikely place,
      a manger –

Who grew up saying
  strange and
    unbelievable
      things.

One thing he said
  sticks clearly
    in my mind;

"I lay down my life
  that I might take
    it again.

No man taketh it from
    me, but
  I lay it down of
      myself.

I have power to lay
  it down and

I have power to take
  it again."

And on that day
  that he lay it
    down

The graves were opened;
  and many bodies
    which slept, arose
      and went into
        the holy city.

"And appeared unto many."

Why not now?

www.ingramcontent.com/pod-product-compliance
Lightning Source LLC
Chambersburg PA
CBHW022011080426
42733CB00007B/563